# Containing Russia
How to Respond to Moscow's
Intervention in U.S. Democracy
and Growing Geopolitical Challenge

**COUNCIL** *on*
**FOREIGN**
**RELATIONS**

Council Special Report No. 80
January 2018

Robert D. Blackwill and Philip H. Gordon

# Containing Russia
How to Respond to Moscow's
Intervention in U.S. Democracy
and Growing Geopolitical Challenge

# Contents

# Foreword

Russia's interference in the 2016 U.S. presidential election constituted an attack on American democracy. No one can know for sure what, if any, effect this attack had on the results of the election. But this question, and others like it, are a distraction. In the words of Senior Fellows Robert D. Blackwill and Philip H. Gordon, the two authors of this new Council Special Report, "The important point is not that Russia changed the outcome of a U.S. presidential election but that it attempted to do so."

The report also makes clear that this attempt by Russia to interfere with American democracy did not take place in a vacuum. To the contrary, it was and is part of a larger political and geopolitical effort designed by Russian President Vladimir Putin "to weaken the United States, divide it from its European allies, and expand Russian influence in Europe, the Middle East, Asia, and beyond."

The authors are unsparing in their assessment of how the current and previous American presidents and their administrations have dealt with the Russian effort to affect the U.S. election, describing their responses as "limited and ineffective." The authors advocate additional measures to better protect U.S. society, punish Russia, and deter Russia and others from continuing to directly interfere in the workings of democracies.

More broadly, the report judges that the United States is currently in a second Cold War with Russia. Consistent with this assessment, the authors recommend what would be tantamount to a new containment policy, one that would include expanded sanctions, electoral and cyber countermeasures, and additional investments in European security. These policy prescriptions come from practitioners who have advised Republican and Democratic presidents and spent their time in government working to build constructive U.S.-Russia relations.

The report is thus nuanced as well as sober. It calls for the United States to confront Russia more robustly, but at the same time it reminds readers that just as it did during the Cold War, the United States should continue to interact with Russia and look for ways to cooperate when it would be in the U.S. national interest.

The Donald J. Trump administration's first National Security Strategy (NSS) identified Russia as a principal challenger to American power, singling out its interference in the domestic political affairs of countries around the world and its attempts to undermine the legitimacy of democracies. The NSS also notes that Russia aims to weaken U.S. influence around the world and divide the United States from its allies and partners. This view has much in common with what is argued in this report; the Trump administration and Congress would be wise to carefully read the policy prescriptions put forward by Blackwill and Gordon and consider making them their own.

**Richard N. Haass**
*President*
Council on Foreign Relations
January 2018

# Acknowledgments

This Council Special Report greatly benefited from comments and input from experts and scholars including Ivo Daalder, Daniel Fried, Laura Rosenberger, Adam Segal, Eugene Steinberg, and Alexander Vershbow. We are grateful to Council on Foreign Relations (CFR) President Richard N. Haass and Senior Vice President and Director of Studies James M. Lindsay for their review and feedback. We also thank Alexander Decina and Theodore Rappleye for contributing research, and the CFR publications team, Patricia Lee Dorff, Julie Hersh, Erik Crouch, and Sumit Poudyal, for their editorial contributions. The analysis and conclusions of the report are the responsibility of the authors alone.

**Robert D. Blackwill** and **Philip H. Gordon**

"Our relations have come to such a pass that no halfway measures will do. . . . I recommend in the strongest terms I can express that I be given some concrete means of showing Soviet officials that their outrageous actions against us are affecting their vital interests."[1]

W. Averell Harriman
U.S. Ambassador to the Soviet Union
April 10, 1945

*Council Special Report*

# Introduction

With each passing week, the evidence of the extent of Russia's interference in the 2016 U.S. presidential election—and in U.S. politics and society more generally—grows. Since at least 2014, in an effort to influence the election and undermine confidence in American democracy, Russia has hacked private American citizens' and organizations' computers to steal information; released that information in ways designed to affect electoral outcomes and divide Americans; planted and disseminated disinformation in U.S. social media; used its state-funded and state-controlled media networks such as RT and Sputnik to spread that disinformation; purchased ads on U.S. social media sites such as Facebook to spread targeted information designed to anger or inspire political and social groups; deployed tens of thousands of bloggers and bots to disseminate disinformation; cooperated with American citizens and possibly even the Donald J. Trump campaign to discredit Trump's opponent in the election; and probed election-related computer systems in at least twenty-one U.S. states.

The United States will never know for certain whether Russia's intervention changed the outcome of the 2016 election. In such a close race—where the result could have been tipped by changing fewer than eighty thousand votes in three states—it is possible, but it is no more provable than an assertion that any other of an almost infinite variety of factors proved decisive. The important point is not that Russia changed the outcome of a U.S. presidential election but that it attempted to do so.

Beyond the attempted election interference, Russia's continued efforts to sow and exacerbate divisions among Americans—using many of the same tools just mentioned—are also unprecedented. Throughout 2017, Moscow continued to fund and direct efforts to fuel racial, religious, and cultural resentments throughout society, pitting Americans against each other and many of their politicians. Whereas physical attacks on the U.S. homeland, such as Pearl Harbor or 9/11, have

3

brought Americans together in a common cause and led them to bolster defenses against such attacks (rather successfully, in fact), attacks on the American sense of national unity could substantially weaken the foundational institutions and shared beliefs that are the essence of the United States and are crucial to its enduring success. The threats of growing domestic strife and diminishing trust in national institutions are as great as any traditional national security threat—with the exception of a nuclear weapons attack—the United States faces today.

Russia's wider challenges to American national interests are also growing. Since Vladimir Putin returned to the presidency in 2012, Moscow has significantly stepped up its efforts to confront the United States and its allies politically and militarily and to counter American influence worldwide. It has invaded and annexed Crimea; intervened in and occupied parts of eastern Ukraine; deployed substantial military forces and undertaken a ruthless bombing campaign in Syria to prop up the Bashar al-Assad regime and defeat the American-supported opposition; significantly expanded its armed forces and deployed missiles in violation of treaty commitments; undertaken large military exercises designed to intimidate East European states; interfered in the political systems of European countries in much the same way it did in the United States; and used the threat of cutting off gas supplies as leverage over the most energy-dependent European states. Putin is a career intelligence officer who is deeply hostile to democratic change anywhere near Russia, paranoid about what he believes to be U.S. efforts to oust him, and resentful of American domination of the post–Cold War world, and he seems to have made it a personal priority to weaken the United States and contest American influence wherever he can.

Neither President Barack Obama nor President Trump—for different reasons—adequately elevated Russia's intervention in the United States to the national priority that it is, or responded to it in a way sufficient to deter Russia or other hostile states from undertaking future attacks. A wide range of additional measures is therefore needed in order to better protect U.S. society and political and electoral systems from further intervention, punish Russia for attacking the United States, and deter Russia and others from continuing to directly interfere in the workings of American and allied democracies. And this more vigorous response to the challenge from Moscow should not be confined to required measures to protect the United States from Russian election tampering. That sort of tit-for-tat U.S. reaction would only encourage Putin to refine his cyber-penetration techniques. Rather, Russia will need to conclude that it is paying a major price in matters important to it for such cyber interference, especially in the area of European security. Only that is likely to cause Moscow and its national-security establishment to cease and desist regarding the functioning of American democracy.

Having worked since the end of the Cold War to build more constructive U.S.-Russian relations (Blackwill in the George H.W. Bush and George W. Bush administrations and Gordon in the Bill Clinton and Barack Obama administrations), we come only reluctantly to the conclusion that the United States needs to confront Russia more robustly. Just as it did during the Cold War, Washington should continue to interact with Moscow, and it should not refrain from practical cooperation or arms-control agreements with Russia whenever such cooperation is in U.S. interests. But Washington also cannot stand by if a foreign adversary not only adopts an agenda of countering U.S. influence throughout the world but also continues to directly strike at the heart of the U.S. political system and society.

# The Russian Intervention

The evidence that Russia interfered in the 2016 U.S. presidential election is overwhelming. As the Office of the Director of National Intelligence (ODNI) put it in January 2017—in a "high confidence" assessment based on highly classified intelligence—Russia conducted an influence campaign that was "designed to undermine public faith in the U.S. democratic process, denigrate Secretary [of State Hillary Rodham] Clinton, and harm her electability and potential presidency."[2] The campaign—which the intelligence community concluded was ordered by President Putin himself—represented "a significant escalation in directness, level of activity, and scope of effort" of "Moscow's longstanding desire to undermine the US-led liberal democratic order" and reflected Putin and the Russian government's "clear preference for President-elect Trump." According to the ODNI report and extensive subsequent investigative reporting, Russia used a wide range of tools to achieve these goals, including the following:

- *Leaking stolen information.* A major tool in the Russian intervention was to hack into the emails of private U.S. citizens and organizations and then release the stolen information in ways designed to influence the outcome of the election. Beginning at least as early as the summer of 2015 (as discovered by the FBI in September 2015), the Russian General Staff Main Intelligence Directorate (GRU) hacked the emails of the Democratic National Committee (DNC) and Clinton campaign chair John Podesta, and then used Russian or Russia-affiliated entities such as WikiLeaks and DCLeaks to release the stolen, and in some cases manipulated, data in a politically targeted manner. A day after the *Washington Post* broke the story of the DNC hack on June 14, 2016, a Russia-affiliated internet persona called Guccifer 2.0 took credit for it, and on July 22—a day before the start of the Democratic National Convention—WikiLeaks published twenty thousand stolen emails, some of which included offensive comments made by leading

DNC figures about Clinton's rival Bernie Sanders. The goal was to anger Sanders supporters and raise questions about the legitimacy of Clinton's nomination.[3]

- *Using Russian media outlets to spread disinformation.* Moscow used Russian media outlets such as RT and Sputnik extensively to publish and promote false and provocative stories designed to denigrate Hillary Clinton and stoke anger among potential Trump supporters as well as Clinton's opponents on the left. RT reportedly spent $190 million per year on programming and focused on Clinton's "leaked emails and accused her of corruption, poor physical and mental health, and ties to Islamic extremism."[4] Other areas of focus, designed to stoke controversy among Trump supporters, included fracking, the Syrian conflict, and movements such as Occupy Wall Street and Black Lives Matter. RT videos spreading allegations that the Clintons were stealing money from their own foundation or that Trump would not be "permitted" to win the election were viewed millions of times. Disinformation included in such videos was often picked up by Trump-supporting media outlets such as Breitbart News, Infowars, and Fox News' *Hannity* and *Fox and Friends*, vastly expanding their reach.

- *Influencing social media debates with trolls and bots.* To reach more people—and artificially boost perceived numbers of users on Facebook and Twitter—Russia used thousands of bots (automated internet accounts) and paid internet trolls to push out disinformation to millions of Americans. According to testimony by Twitter executives in October 2017, more than thirty thousand Russia-linked accounts generated 1.4 million tweets during the final two months of the campaign.[5] Russian Facebook pages including Being Patriotic, Secured Borders, and Blacktivist picked up controversial issues from conservative or liberal websites and promoted them to feed outrage on subjects such as race, religion, and immigration. For example, when Being Patriotic posted a message rallying Americans against proposals to expand refugee settlements in the United States, it was liked, shared, or otherwise interacted with by more than 750,000 Facebook users.[6] This Russia-promoted information, frequently further disseminated by U.S. media outlets, often included extensive praise for President Putin and criticism of his enemies.

- *Using social media advertising.* The Russian intervention also involved a highly coordinated disinformation campaign of ad purchases on Facebook, Google, and YouTube. In October 2017, Facebook reported that nearly 126 million people had been exposed to content tied to Russia-linked accounts over a two-year period. Much of this advertising was paid for by the St. Petersburg-based Internet Research Agency (IRA), a secretive firm closely tied to Russian intelligence and known for spreading Russian propaganda. According to Facebook, IRA—likely bankrolled by the Russian oligarch and Putin ally Yevgeny Prigozhin—paid $100,000 for three thousand ads to promote content on its platform, and the posts likely reached about ten million people.[7] In buying the ads and using them for political purposes, Russia exploited a loophole in the 2002 Bipartisan Campaign Reform Act, which requires disclosure of purchasers of campaign ads and forbids foreign nationals from purchasing such ads but whose definition of "electioneering communications" covers only broadcast, cable, and satellite communications—not social media.[8]

- *Targeting voting systems.* According to the U.S. Department of Homeland Security, Russia targeted presidential election–related voting systems in at least twenty-one states, including swing states Florida, Ohio, Pennsylvania, Virginia, and Wisconsin. Although most of these attacks were considered "preparatory activity" and most attempts to infiltrate systems failed, two states (Arizona and Illinois) confirmed that attackers did compromise their voting systems.[9] Investigators said that as many as thirty-nine states were targeted in attempts to manipulate and sabotage voter data.[10]

- *Forging documents.* Russia allegedly produced a fake intelligence document designed to suggest collusion between the Clinton campaign and then Attorney General Loretta Lynch. Officials say that although the FBI knew the document was fake, concerns about its existence could nonetheless have contributed to then FBI Director James Comey's decision to make a highly unusual July 2016 statement harshly criticizing Clinton for her email practices even while announcing she would not be indicted.[11]

- *Cooperating with the Trump campaign.* The degree of possible Russian collusion with the Trump campaign is still being investigated, but that Moscow sought at least some cooperation with numerous people affiliated with the campaign is a near certainty. As early as spring 2016 (before the U.S. intelligence community was even aware of Russian efforts), campaign foreign policy advisor George Papadopoulos was reporting to senior campaign officials that Russia had "dirt" and "thousands of Hillary Clinton's emails" and was exploring how to use them.[12] On June 3, 2016, Trump's son and advisor Donald J. Trump Jr. was offered "official documents and information" that would allegedly incriminate Clinton. A few days later, Trump Jr., campaign chairman Paul Manafort (later indicted for corruptly receiving money from a Russia-backed political party in Ukraine), and Trump senior advisor and son-in-law Jared Kushner met in secret with Natalia Veselnitskaya, the Kremlin-affiliated lawyer who Trump Jr. had been told would deliver the incriminating information.[13] In the weeks that followed, Trump promised to hold a news conference about Clinton's alleged wrongdoings and began to publicly praise WikiLeaks, and on July 27 called on Russia to release more Clinton emails.[14] On July 7 and 8, Trump foreign policy advisor Carter Page traveled to Moscow, where he met with at least one senior Russian official—contrary to later denials—and reported to senior campaign staff that he received "incredible insights and outreach" and signals of Russia's "desire to work together."[15] On August 21, Trump advisor Roger Stone posted tweets indicating that he had advance knowledge of an upcoming leak of John Podesta's emails.[16] And throughout October 2016, Trump Jr. had multiple online conversations with WikiLeaks about how stolen documents could be used to embarrass Clinton, some of which were followed up by tweets or comments by candidate Trump (and Trump Jr.) using the material.[17] More important than the degree to which senior members of the Trump campaign, or Trump himself, directly colluded with the Russians is that Russia not only sought to influence the outcome of an American election but also tried to work with Americans in an effort to do so.

Russia's intervention in the 2016 presidential election was an unprecedented event in U.S. history. Moscow, during the Cold War, at times attempted to discredit candidates perceived to be hostile to Soviet interests, but it never undertook such a vast, determined, multifaceted effort to affect an electoral outcome in the United States. In the words of Admiral Michael S. Rogers, director of the National Security Agency, "There shouldn't be any doubts in anybody's mind: This was not something that was done casually; this was not something that was done by chance; this was not a target that was selected purely arbitrarily. This was a conscious effort by a nation-state to attempt to achieve a specific effect."[18]

# The U.S. Response—
# Obama, Trump, and Congress

Considering the gravity and consequences of the Russian intervention, the U.S. response so far has been limited and ineffective. The Obama administration was slow to realize the full extent of the Russian operation, and when it did it remained reluctant to react, announcing only a limited set of retaliatory measures after the election was over. In the run-up to that election, Obama was concerned that public accusations of Russian interference would be perceived as an attempt to discredit the Trump candidacy (an accusation Trump ended up making anyway) and that retaliation could set off a mutually devastating cyber escalation with Russia—which could disproportionately hurt the United States because of its greater openness and reliance on technology. These concerns led the administration to avoid retaliating in a manner proportionate to the intervention, or even from publicly highlighting the seriousness of the Russian intervention to the degree it deserved.

The Obama administration did make some effort to draw attention to Russia's actions and took several steps in response. The first was an effort to win bipartisan support from Congress to jointly publicize Russia's actions, hoping that a bipartisan response would avoid the perception that the administration was acting on behalf of the Democratic candidate. However, when top administration officials sought support for a joint approach to the issue from a group of congressional leaders, presenting them with classified evidence of Russia's DNC and other cyber intrusions, they were rebuffed. Senate Majority Leader Mitch McConnell (R-KY) in particular expressed doubts about the underlying intelligence and warned that he would accuse the administration of partisanship if it publicly challenged the Russians.[19] The Trump campaign was deeply hostile to any implication that it was receiving support from Russia, and congressional Republicans were unwilling to do anything that could help Trump's opponent, regardless of how much evidence was presented. Without bipartisan support, and (wrongly) convinced that Clinton would win the election anyway, the Obama administration refrained from a high-profile public response. The administration did proceed on its own with efforts to shore up the national voting infrastructure, but here too it faced resistance—this time from state-level officials who opposed administration actions on the issue as an undue assault on states' rights.[20]

The Obama administration also took steps to warn the Russians that consequences would follow if they did not stand down. On August 4, 2016, then CIA Director John Brennan told his Russian counterpart, Alexander Bortnikov, that "if you go down this road, it's going to have serious consequences not only for the bilateral relationship but for our ability to work with Russia on any issue, because it is an assault on our democracy."[21] Obama conveyed a similar message directly to Putin in September (at a Group of Twenty summit in China), and such messages continued in numerous channels until Election Day.[22] Some Obama officials believe this messaging deterred further Russian covert action—or at least an attack on Election Day voting itself—but ongoing Russian activities into 2017 suggest that its effect, if any, was limited.

The administration also eventually agreed, even in the absence of bipartisan support, to make public what it knew (though the government's knowledge of Putin's role was omitted, and Obama himself did not make the statement lest it be perceived to be political). On October 7, 2016, the Department of Homeland Security and the ODNI stated the U.S. intelligence community's confidence that "the Russian government directed the recent compromises of emails from U.S. persons and institutions" and that "only Russia's senior-most officials could have authorized these activities."[23] Designed to heighten public attention on the Russian hack, the statement was immediately overshadowed by the release of a video of Trump bragging about sexually assaulting women and, less than an hour after that, by WikiLeaks' publication of thousands of Podesta's emails. The release of the Trump tape not only drew public attention away from the intelligence community's Russia statement but also, by appearing to make a Trump victory even less likely, could have led the administration to conclude that further efforts to respond to Russia could wait until after the election.

It was not until nearly two months after Trump's victory that the Obama administration actually responded to the Russian intervention. On December 29, Obama announced that the United States would expel thirty-five "intelligence operatives" and imposed new sanctions on Russian state agencies and individuals suspected in the hacks of U.S. computer systems. The new sanctions targeted the GRU (Russia's military spy agency) and the Federal Security Service (FSB, the successor to the KGB), as well as four GRU officials and three companies believed to have supported cyber operations. At the same time, Obama ordered the closure of two Russian-owned facilities on Maryland's Eastern Shore and New York's Long Island ostensibly established as recreational facilities for embassy personnel and their families but in fact used for espionage. Obama described this set of measures as "a necessary and appropriate response to efforts to harm U.S. interest," but they appear to have had little effect on Russia's ongoing activities.[24]

The Trump administration has done even less. Trump opposed Obama's December 2016 retaliatory measures, calling on "our country to move on to bigger and better things."[25] Indeed, far from responding to Russia's intervention, Trump has refused even to acknowledge that it happened, repeatedly calling the allegations of electoral interference a "hoax" and accusing Clinton supporters of making them up.[26] During the campaign, Trump repeatedly said that he did not think it happened and (somewhat contradictorily) suggested that it could have been done by Russia but perhaps also by China or "somebody sitting on their bed that weighs four hundred pounds."[27] In July 2017, Trump even proposed working with Russia to create a joint cybersecurity unit; although the unit was never created, the initiative underscored Trump's vision of Russia as a potential cyber partner rather than an adversary that had attacked the United States.[28] And on November 11, 2017, despite the assessment of his own CIA director that Russia did interfere, as spelled out in a January 2017 joint intelligence report, Trump still claimed that report was produced by partisan "hacks" and asserted that he believed Putin's repeated denials of interference were sincere.[29]

Throughout his campaign and presidency, for reasons difficult to explain, Trump has in fact demonstrated a curious affinity for Russia in general and Putin specifically, often praising the Russian leader and rarely challenging Russian policy positions. Whereas Trump's default attitude toward virtually every other country in the world is highly critical and he insists that the United States has been getting a "bad deal," he has consistently shown sympathy and understanding for Russian perspectives and suggested it would be "nice if we could just get along."[30] He even relativized Putin's alleged killings of journalists and other opposition figures, asserting in a television interview that "our country does plenty of killing too."[31] During his campaign, Trump and his team softened the language on Ukraine in the Republican Party platform, expressed openness to recognizing Russia's annexation of Crimea, called the North Atlantic Treaty Organization (NATO) obsolete, questioned NATO's Article 5 commitment to collective defense, and made a priority of working with Russia in Syria.[32] In November 2017, Trump was still saying he hoped to find a way to lift sanctions on Russia to promote cooperation, and insisting on Twitter that "having a good relationship with Russia is a good thing, not a bad thing. . . . I want to solve North Korea, Syria, Ukraine, terrorism, and Russia can greatly help!"[33]

In the absence of a vigorous response by the Trump administration, it has fallen to Congress to take the lead in responding to the Russian intervention. Three congressional committees—House Intelligence, Senate Select Intelligence, and Senate Judiciary—are currently conducting investigations, and, despite deep partisan splits within them, all at least accept the premise that Russian intervention occurred and steps should be taken to ensure that it never happens again.

In July 2017, Congress also passed legislation designed to punish Russia for hacking the election. The Countering America's Adversaries Through Sanctions Act of 2017 (CAATSA) codified into law sanctions imposed by previous administrations so that Trump could not lift them without congressional consent.[34] CAATSA imposes new sanctions that can be used in response to cyber intrusions and expands sectoral sanctions by decreasing the allowable term of extensions of debt and credit to Russian banks and energy companies operating in those sectors. CAATSA also extends worldwide the restrictions on Russian firms involved in "special" oil production technology (for shale, deepwater, and Arctic offshore projects) and authorizes the Treasury Department to add the railway or metals and mining sectors to the list of potentially sanctionable sectors. Finally, the law mandates cybersecurity sanctions against those helping Russia undermine the cybersecurity of any democratic institution or government (including U.S. institutions).[35]

Although CAATSA gives the Trump administration new and potentially effective tools to punish Russia for its transgressions and deter future ones, there are reasons to doubt that the administration plans to use those tools. Trump initially opposed the bill and only signed it in the face of overwhelming congressional pressure, while issuing a signing statement calling it "seriously flawed."[36] The administration then dragged its feet on implementation, failing to meet deadlines for identifying the Russian defense and intelligence officials who could be subject to sanctions; then, in October 2017, the State Department announced that it was closing its Coordinator for Sanctions Policy office and transferring those responsibilities to a mid-level official on the policy planning staff.[37]

# The Wider Russian Challenge

The Russian effort to destabilize the United States does not take place in a vacuum. Rather, it stems from the Russian president's strongly held view—shared by a wide range of Russians—that the spread of U.S. regional and global hegemony since the end of the Cold War threatens Russian vital national interests and deprives Russia of its rightful place on the world stage. A career intelligence officer who served in East Germany during the Cold War, Putin has always seen the relationship with the United States in largely zero-sum terms. In 2007, in a famous speech at the Munich Security Conference, he complained that "one state and, of course, first and foremost the United States, has overstepped its national borders in every way" and expressed his hostility to a U.S.-led unipolar world.[38] Putin views American foreign policies such as the enlargement of NATO, European missile defense deployments, and support for democracy around the world (and particularly in Russia) as direct threats to Russia's national interests. His goals are to weaken the United States, divide it from its European allies, and expand Russian influence in Europe, the Middle East, Asia, and beyond.

Putin's pursuit of this agenda has been particularly vigorous since his return to the presidency for a third term in 2012. As prime minister from 2008 to 2012, Putin tolerated then President Dmitry Medvedev's "reset" of relations with the Obama administration but ultimately viewed that experience as a failure that only enabled the United States to expand its global and regional hegemony. Despite Obama's efforts to improve the bilateral relationship, Putin saw ongoing U.S. support for NATO, the deployment of new missile defense systems in Poland and Romania, U.S. assistance to the Syrian opposition, and NATO's military intervention in Libya—taking advantage of Russia's abstention on the UN Security Council resolution that authorized it—as inconsistent with better relations and contrary to Russia's national interest. When, in the summer of 2012, the U.S. Congress passed the Magnitsky Act—

a set of tough sanctions on eighteen Russian officials involved in the torture and death in prison of Russian human rights whistle-blower Sergei
Magnitsky—Putin responded harshly, with matching sanctions on an
equivalent number of Americans and a ban on all American adoptions
of Russian children.[39]

Russia's efforts to defend its perceived interests—and to counter
American influence—have since been extensive. Since reassuming
the presidency, Putin has continued to increase military spending, to
around $70 billion or 5.3 percent of gross domestic product (GDP),
the highest percentage spent on defense since the Russian Federation
emerged in 1991.[40] In 2014, when Ukrainians rebelled against their government for backing away from closer ties with the European Union,
Russia invaded and annexed Crimea and deployed large numbers of
regular and irregular soldiers in eastern Ukraine, where they remain
today. In Syria, hostile to regime change and determined to prevent
the United States from expanding its influence in the Middle East,
Russia supplied the Assad regime with significant funding and weap-
onry before intervening directly in September 2015 with its own armed
forces to lead military operations on Assad's behalf, which successfully
altered the battlefield balance of power. In Afghanistan, Russia has
openly admitted to sharing intelligence with the Afghan Taliban since
2015, ostensibly to fight the self-proclaimed Islamic State, and officials
in the Afghan and U.S. governments, including Generals John Nich-
olson and Joseph Votel, have suggested that Russia is providing the
Taliban with lethal weapons.[41] Russia has also beefed up its military
presence in the Arctic, Northern Europe, and the Caucasus; expanded
military exercises, including the September 2017 Zapad exercise of
more than seventy thousand troops in western Russia; sought to interfere in European elections much as it did in the United States; launched
cyberattacks on information systems in the Baltic states and Eastern
Europe; built up its nuclear forces; and deployed new mid-range missiles, in breach of the 1987 Intermediate-Range Nuclear Forces (INF)
Treaty.[42] Taken together, this set of policies constitutes the most significant—and successful—Russian effort to contain American power and
influence since the end of the Cold War.

In this context, Putin's motivations for seeking to destabilize the
United States—and to promote the election of Donald Trump over
Hillary Clinton—are not hard to fathom. As secretary of state from
2009 to 2013, Clinton made clear that the Obama administration's

reset did not mean that the United States would back away from its traditional support for NATO allies, missile defense, or democracy and human rights in Europe. In particular, Putin resented Clinton's comments in December 2011—as thousands of Russians demonstrated against what they alleged were rigged Duma elections—that "the Russian people . . . deserve the right to have their voices heard and . . . leaders who are accountable to them."[43] Whereas for Clinton this was a fairly routine American expression of support for democracy and free speech, Putin saw it as a signal to the protesters and proof that Clinton and the United States were determined to threaten his rule—just as they had supported the protests that had toppled dictators in Georgia and Ukraine in 2003 and 2004 and in Tunisia, Egypt, Libya, and Yemen in 2011 and 2012.

Thus, while Clinton campaigned for policies that would stand in the way of Russian objectives—policies such as arming Ukraine, a no-fly zone in Syria, NATO enlargement, and U.S. support for democracy—a Trump presidency must have seemed highly desirable to Putin. For seventy years, U.S. presidents from both parties saw the preservation of world order and containment of Russian expansion as fundamental to American interests and had largely succeeded in achieving both. It is no wonder that Putin saw the 2016 election as an opportunity to end that long tradition and that he devoted the resources of the Russian state to doing so.

# Recommendations

There is no doubt that Putin ordered the Russian government to mount an unprecedented effort to undermine U.S. democracy and influence the outcome of the 2016 U.S. presidential election on behalf of Donald Trump. In effect, Moscow's ultimate objective was regime change in the United States. There is also little doubt that Russian interventions continue—both to influence upcoming elections and to divide Americans, fanning the flames of cultural, racial, and class resentment and seeking to delegitimize institutions, the free press, and elected officials. Moscow is without question currently seeking to learn the lessons of its influence campaign and refining techniques that, if not stopped, it will use again in 2018 and 2020. As former Director of National Intelligence James Clapper put it, "The Russians succeeded beyond their wildest expectations."[44] They will almost certainly seek to build on that success if they are not prevented or deterred from doing so.

Some analysts argue that despite this extraordinary Russian attack on the core of the American democratic system, other and larger equities in the U.S.-Russia relationship should be protected.[45] The importance of the full range of bilateral political, economic, and strategic issues is not in dispute, not least the paramount importance of avoiding a nuclear clash, unlikely as that is. But none of these issues should prevent the United States from reacting strongly to Russia's destabilizing behavior. Failing to respond would encourage Moscow, using ever more advanced technology, to repeat and expand its interference in U.S. and allied democratic processes and its corrosive attempts to turn Americans against one another. The need for nuclear stability does not seem to have constrained Putin and his agenda of undermining U.S. power and prestige whenever and wherever he can, and it should not prevent the United States from reacting to that agenda.

There is no doubt that Putin ordered what George W. Bush has rightly called "a sustained attempt by a hostile power to feed and exploit our country's divisions."[46] Moscow sought the election of a man who does not share the fundamental strategic perspectives of every U.S. president since Harry S. Truman.

Russian interference in American democratic processes and norms should put the United States on a different path regarding its relations with Moscow. Russia's intervention should not be seen as just another of many stumbles in U.S.-Russia relations over the decades but as a historic turning point. No matter how adroit U.S. diplomacy, it is now clear no benign deal is to be had with Putin. He is ruthlessly determined to do what he can to undermine U.S. foreign policy and American democratic society.

The following policy prescriptions are therefore designed in the first instance to deter Russia from again stoking disunity in the United States by making clear to the Kremlin and to its national security apparatus the significant cost of their activities. The United States should take measures to strengthen its defenses against such attacks and to increase the costs of past and potential future interventions, and should embark on a full-scale reinvigoration of U.S. European security policy, expressly and publicly tied to Putin's across-the-board destabilizing policies. NATO is immeasurably stronger than Russia diplomatically, economically, and militarily. It is time for this to be demonstrated.

Indeed, because of Russian policies, the United States and its European treaty allies regrettably are now forced to adopt a policy of containment to protect the sovereignty, security, and democracy of all NATO members, because Moscow seeks to undermine all three. Put differently, currently no acceptable grand bargain with Putin is possible that would produce more responsible Russian behavior regarding European security and the West. Rather, Putin seems determined to exploit what he regards as the moral and philosophical weakness of the democracies to Russia's strategic advantage. To permit him to do so would produce a profound geopolitical shift in the global balance of power and put Western values and national interests on a downward slope. That cannot be allowed to happen.

Thus, the United States should work to advance the comprehensive policy prescriptions that follow.

*Expanded Sanctions*

- Impose additional sanctions on Russia and its government officials specifically for interference in the 2016 election. The minimal sanctions so far imposed have failed to send a sufficiently powerful message to Moscow. The passage of CAATSA, which required the imposition of sanctions on various Russian officials and defense and intelligence agencies for their election interference, was an important first step, but the Trump administration has unfortunately failed to use the tools now at its disposal. It should approve asset freezes and visa bans on the additional Russian officials now known to be involved in election interference.

- Extend similar sanctions on Russian organizations active in election interference, including "troll farms" and their sources of financing.

- Work closely with European allies to ensure a united front in deterring companies from doing business with the Russian defense and intelligence sectors. CAATSA required the administration to choose from a menu of sanctions on persons engaging in "significant transactions" with the Russian defense or intelligence sector, and on October 26 the Treasury Department's Office of Foreign Assets Control (OFAC) identified entities subject to those sanctions. The OFAC list includes Russian aircraft manufacturer Sukhoi, state arms exporter Rosoboronexport, airplane manufacturer Tupolev, defense and industrial conglomerate Rostec, and the Russian foreign intelligence service (SVR). The existence of this list of entities alone will be costly to Russia because companies will not want to risk sanctions by making "significant investments," but the administration should not hesitate to impose those sanctions—selectively—if tested.[47]

- Separate the sanctions imposed in response to Russia's aggression against Ukraine from election-related (and other) sanctions to maintain the ability to remove sanctions if Russia agrees to a settlement compatible with the Minsk accords that restores Ukrainian sovereignty over Donbas.

*Electoral and Cyber Countermeasures*

- Promptly and fully implement the administration's May 11, 2017, executive order to strengthen the cybersecurity of federal networks and critical infrastructure so that agencies can better detect, monitor, and mitigate attacks as quickly as possible.[48] Declassify enough information about the nature of Russian hacking, and provide substantial funding and support from the Department of Homeland Security, to share with the private sector so that it can do the same.[49]

- Encourage state and local election boards to keep paper backups of ballots and voter registration records and to limit access to election systems to qualified vendors, secure voter registration logs, and improve security information sharing about potential threats.[50]

- Invest in education and recruitment for professionals who can take cybersecurity positions in the U.S. government, and create a fellowship program to attract cybersecurity specialists modeled on the Centers for Disease Control and Prevention's Epidemic Intelligence Service. Invest in Department of Defense and private-sector research that could produce breakthrough cyber weapons for the United States.[51]

- Support legislation to update campaign finance laws to cover a broader range of online activity, enhance transparency requirements, and prevent political spending by foreign nationals. New laws should require digital platforms to create a public database of political ads and provide users access to information about paid political ads, including who paid for the ads and who the target audience is.[52] The administration should also create and apply regulations to online or media activities similar to the Foreign Agents Registration Act, which requires transparency in lobbying. Americans advancing a foreign political influence campaign through vehicles such as RT should not be treated differently from those being paid directly by foreign governments.[53]

- Support bipartisan nongovernmental-organization efforts, such as the German Marshall Fund of the United States' Alliance for Securing Democracy platform, to help combat disinformation and expose the fact that Russian propaganda networks such as RT and Sputnik are not legitimate journalism outlets.[54]

- Selectively declassify intelligence demonstrating Russian interference in U.S. domestic politics.

- Work with major social media platforms to develop a voluntary code of conduct to more actively police their networks for disinformation, false news stories, botnets, and false-flag advertising—identifying, labeling, and blocking them where appropriate. Facebook's decision to create a portal to help people identify ads from Russia's Internet Research Agency, Twitter's ban of RT and Sputnik from advertising, and Google's consideration of de-ranking RT and Sputnik are all steps in the right direction.[55]

- Privately convey to Moscow the U.S. readiness to covertly release the financial information of Russian government leaders involved in hacking, and to release other embarrassing information about Putin and his cronies, including the extent of corruption in Russian business. Credibly threatening such actions would give Putin an incentive and opportunity to refrain from future interventions in U.S. elections, whereas taking those actions now would do the opposite—escalating the crisis and giving up potential leverage without getting anything positive in return.

- Clarify to the Russian leadership that these U.S. measures are defensive in nature and not designed to change the Russian regime—a fear Putin has harbored for years (and which was exacerbated by the 2016 publication of the Panama Papers, which Putin blamed on the United States).[56] The United States should make clear that it will continue to support free and fair elections, freedom of speech, and the rule of law in Russia, as it does all around the world. But it will respect Russia's sovereign right to hold those elections free of outside manipulation with illicit means—just as it expects Russia to respect the United States' right to do the same.

*European Security*

- Recognize that an effective response to Russia's interference requires close cooperation with European allies to bolster NATO's defense and deterrence posture, building on the measures adopted at the Wales (2014) and Warsaw (2016) summits.

- Do not recognize the annexation of Crimea and maintain the sanctions imposed. Russia might never return Crimea to Ukraine, but softening the Crimea sanctions regime would confirm Putin's view that the West will eventually accept his brutal dismemberment of Ukraine. In the same spirit, do not join Russia and only a handful of other countries in recognizing South Ossetia and Abkhazia as independent states but instead support Georgia's efforts to peacefully reestablish its national boundaries recognized by international law.

- If Russia does not fully implement the February 2015 Minsk II agreement or any successor to it, work with European partners to expand sanctions to cover additional Russian officials and specific firms, and further limit Russian access to Western loans and technology. The expansion of sanctions to the defense, mining, and energy sectors is specifically authorized in CAATSA, and the Trump administration should not hesitate to implement such sanctions. If this first expansion of sanctions does not work, further limit access to Western loans and financial services, cancel investments in existing projects, impose sanctions on mining and machinery as defined in CAATSA, and urge allies to embargo all Russian military sales and military imports from Russia.[57] Remove the sanctions related to eastern Ukraine only if the Minsk II deal is enacted, and do not remove Crimea-related sanctions even if Minsk II is successfully implemented.[58] Moscow's strategy toward Ukraine and the Minsk II negotiations is clear: keep talking while militarily propping up the rebels in eastern Ukraine and trying to undermine the Ukrainian state. Infinite patience on NATO's part regarding Minsk II is yet another misreading of Putin's fundamental objectives in Russian foreign policy. He aims to reestablish control over Russia's immediate neighbors, and the West should stop being a naive party to that destabilizing objective, beginning with Ukraine.

- Maintain the numbers of permanent U.S. forces currently in Europe and urge NATO allies to do the same. Although the Obama administration reversed planned troop reductions after the 2014 seizure of Crimea, the number of active-duty personnel in Europe remains at approximately sixty thousand, lower than at any point since the end of the Cold War.[59] The antiquated concept of reducing U.S. troop levels in Europe based on what turned out to be unrealistic hopes and dreams has been overtaken by the renewed Russian threat. Sadly, NATO governments should recognize that the foundations of European security have changed for the worse because of Putin's neo-imperial policies and that the West requires a new strategy to deal with Moscow.

- Deploy permanently an additional armored combat brigade in Poland and maintain permanent multinational battalions in the Baltic states, backed up with a greater capacity for rapid reinforcement and sustainability. Also position more equipment close to the eastern flank, establish effective air-defense capabilities in the Baltic states, and—together with allies—deploy the air, maritime, and anti-submarine warfare capabilities needed to counter Russia's ability to impede NATO reinforcements. Such measures would provide needed reassurance to NATO east European allies that the alliance's Article 5 remains sacrosanct, a commitment on the part of the United States that some allies and probably Putin now question.[60]

- Allocate additional funds to NATO programs, including the Euro-pean Reassurance Initiative, to improve alliance logistical networks. This step would allow NATO to move troops and supplies eastward quickly in the event of a Russian attack and could mitigate Russian anti-access/area denial near the Baltic states. This along with the other measures enumerated here would send a clear signal to the GRU that Kremlin interference in the U.S. election has substan-tially bolstered NATO's common defense and introduced a series of enhanced challenges to Russian military planning.

- Help train residents of the Baltic states to resist any attempted Rus-sian intervention or occupation. The Baltic states too often feel mostly on their own in protecting their territories from their large predatory neighbor to the east. NATO should launch a comprehen-sive initiative to bring the Baltic nations securely within the alliance shield, both tangibly and psychologically.

- Conduct more NATO naval exercises in the Baltic and Black Seas, as well as the North Atlantic Ocean, and improve NATO reconnais-sance capabilities to track Russian exercises in those waters as well as to enhance NATO anti-submarine warfare capabilities against Russia. Increase the numbers of modern sensors and aircraft, sub-marines, and surface ships, in conjunction with NATO allies and non-NATO partners in the region. The alliance needs to move into a new and robust phase of defending the seas around Europe in all their aspects.

- Work with NATO allies to improve information-sharing capabili-ties with U.S. and British cyberwarfare units and to develop a com-prehensive cyber strategy to combat Russian hacking. The alliance should embark on a major overhaul of its cyber capabilities and vulnerabilities. In addition to bolstering cyber defenses and "cyber embassies" to supply attacked NATO countries with digital services from other NATO countries, it should develop offensive cyber capa-bilities to block Russian communication lines, intelligence collection, and command and control centers in the event of an attack. Ensure that offensive cyber methods remain classified to inflate Russian cal-culations of the costs of attacking a NATO country. Given Russian activities, NATO is years behind where it needs to be.[61]

- Maintain at least the six U.S. fighter squadrons currently deployed on air bases in Europe, and invest further in the F-35A (to replace at least two F-15 squadrons) and in long-range air-to-air missiles.[62] NATO needs to command the skies over Europe.

- Provide additional defensive support to Ukraine, including counter-battery radars, reconnaissance drones, secure communications, and armored vehicles. Ukraine should not be encouraged to seek a military victory over Russia, which it cannot achieve, but it can be helped to better protect itself and increase the costs to Russia of its occupation. Additional military support to Ukraine, including anti-tank weapons, could be provided if Russia refuses to implement a peace agreement or expands its occupation, and as Ukrainian political and military reforms progress.

- Remove U.S. budget sequestration caps on defense spending. This is long overdue to promote European security and the broader U.S. global security role.

- Continue to implement the European Phased Adaptive Approach to deal with missile threats to Europe from beyond the NATO theater. To bolster NATO air and missile defenses against Russian short- and medium-range ballistic and cruise missile threats, invest and urge allies to invest in local European radar systems, and continue to deploy Patriot Advanced Capability-3 (PAC-3) missiles in Poland and the Baltic states. Any U.S. or NATO hesitation on missile defense because of Russian opposition only feeds Putin's expansionist appetite.

- Continue to remove restrictions on U.S. oil and gas exports to Europe to reduce European reliance on Russian gas, such as by expediting the reviews of smaller liquefied natural gas exports.[63] Encourage the construction of gas pipelines that avoid Russia (such as from Turkmenistan through Azerbaijan and Turkey to Europe).[64] Urge NATO allies and other EU member states to pursue alternatives to the Nord Stream 2 pipeline from Russia, including by facilitating their purchases of liquid natural gas from elsewhere.

- Coordinate all these initiatives concerning Russia's aggressive behavior with European partners.

- Publicize Russian human rights abuses within its borders and in neighboring countries, impose more sanctions on Russian officials who commit abuses, and urge European countries to introduce legislation similar to the U.S. Magnitsky Act.

*Conventional Forces and the Organization for Security and Cooperation in Europe*

- Abrogate the Treaty on Conventional Armed Forces in Europe (CFE) if Russia continues to violate it.
- Maintain the NATO-Russia Founding Act and use it as a channel for dialogue unless Russia takes military or other seriously damaging action against a NATO member.[65] Enact standards that reduce the risk of military accidents, drop legal limits on U.S.-Russia military-to-military contact to discuss safety at lower levels, and remain in dialogue with Russia about conventional arms control, the inadequacy of the current CFE Treaty, and the prevention of military accidents.
- Update the Vienna Document as soon as possible to outline confidence- and security-building measures, including lowering the thresholds for requiring observers to be present at military exercises and giving Organization for Security and Cooperation in Europe monitors greater access to regional European conflicts.[66]
- Seek to remain in the Open Skies Treaty, but leave if Russia does not move back into compliance, because Russia benefits more from the treaty than the United States does.

*Intermediate-Range Nuclear Forces Treaty*

- Publicly declare that Russia is in material breach of the INF Treaty.
- Demand that Russia quickly and verifiably move back into compliance with the INF Treaty and withdraw from it if Russia does not comply.
- Do not fund a new ground-launched cruise missile that would violate the INF Treaty because this move would be met with political resistance from allies; use air and sea missiles instead.
- Invest heavily in cruise missile defense, including by deploying the PAC-3, to protect transportation and logistical networks, preventing Russia from paralyzing a NATO military response with a missile banned by the INF Treaty.[67]
- Use economic and diplomatic methods to prevent other countries from purchasing Russian missiles that violate the INF Treaty, and signal that the United States would be willing to block other arms sales in the future.[68]

## New START

- Invest in additional programs as needed to modernize the U.S. nuclear arsenal.

- Stay in the Treaty on Measures for the Further Reduction and Limitation of Strategic Offensive Arms (New START), and if violations occur, use the treaty's provisions to address them.

- Consider extending New START by five years, to 2026, even before the treaty is fully implemented in 2018, before increased tensions make further arms control negotiations difficult or impossible.

# Conclusion

The United States is currently in a second Cold War with Russia. Policy prescriptions reflecting a U.S. containment policy logically follow that unfortunate reality. President Putin, in launching an encompassing attack on U.S. democracy and opposing U.S. policies around the world, has demonstrated beyond a doubt that he will not be a U.S. partner, strategically or tactically, in the period ahead. Rather, Putin has apparently concluded that a larger Russian regional and global role depends on the decline of American power projection. Given its innate advantages and the strength of its alliances, the United States can successfully meet this challenge from Moscow unless Washington succumbs to internal divisions and alliance mismanagement.

There is obviously some question as to whether President Trump—who refuses even to acknowledge the reality of Russian interference—would approve such policies to deal with Russia's deeply destabilizing behavior. Prospects do not seem promising at present, but this could change. After all, Secretary of State Rex Tillerson, Secretary of Defense Jim Mattis, and National Security Advisor H. R. McMaster have made public statements consistent with the analysis in this report.

Tillerson has stressed that "there is clear evidence of Russia meddling in democratic elections in the U.S. and Europe" and argued that "we, together with our friends in Europe, recognize the active threat of a recently resurgent Russia."[69] Mattis has said, "Right now I would just say there's very little doubt that they [the Russians] have either interfered or they have attempted to interfere in a number of elections in the democracies," and that he "would consider the principal threats, to start with, [to be] Russia."[70] And McMaster has described the attack on the election as a "very sophisticated campaign of subversion and disinformation and propaganda that is ongoing every day in an effort to break apart Europe and to pit political groups against each other ... to sow dissension and conspiracy theories." He has stated, "Revisionist

powers Russia and China are subverting the post–World War II political, economic, and security orders to advance their own interests at
our expense and at the expense of our allies."[71] Moreover, the Trump
administration's National Security Strategy, published on December
18, 2017, explicitly states that "actors such as Russia are using information tools in an attempt to undermine the legitimacy of democracies"
and that "Russia challenge[s] American power, influence, and interests,
attempting to erode American security and prosperity."[72] These are
positions with which we heartily agree.

Although we are not optimistic, we hope that President Trump will
eventually listen to the strong and consistent views of his three most
important foreign policy advisors.

# Endnotes

1. William Averell Harriman, unsent State Department cable, April 10, 1945, quoted in Walter Isaacson and Evan Thomas, *The Wise Men: Six Friends and the World They Made* (New York: Simon & Schuster, 1986), 248.
2. Office of the Director of National Intelligence, "Background to 'Assessing Russian Activities and Intentions in Recent US Elections': The Analytic Process and Cyber Incident Attribution," January 6, 2017, https://dni.gov/files/documents/ICA_2017_01.pdf.
3. Ellen Nakashima, "Russian Government Hackers Penetrated DNC, Stole Opposition Research on Trump," *Washington Post*, June 14, 2016, https://washingtonpost.com /world/national-security/russian-government-hackers-penetrated-dnc-stole -opposition-research-on-trump/2016/06/14/cf006cb4-316e-11e6-8ff7-7b6c1998b7a0 _story.html; Charlie Savage, "Assange, Avowed Foe of Clinton, Timed Email Release for Democratic Convention," *New York Times*, June 26, 2016, https://nytimes .com/2016/07/27/us/politics/assange-timed-wikileaks-release-of-democratic-emails -to-harm-hillary-clinton.html; Office of the Director of National Intelligence, "Assessing Russian Activities and Intentions in Recent U.S. Elections," January 6, 2017, https://dni.gov/files/documents/ICA_2017_01.pdf. The tactic was consistent with earlier Russian use of hacked information, such as the release of the Nuland-Pyatt conversation about Ukraine in early 2014 to sow divisions with Europeans. See Doina Chiacu and Arshad Mohammed, "Leaked Audio Reveals Embarrassing U.S. Exchange on Ukraine, EU," Reuters, February 6, 2014, https://reuters.com/article /us-usa-ukraine-tape/leaked-audio-reveals-embarrassing-u-s-exchange-on-ukraine-eu -idUSBREA1601G20140207.
4. Office of the Director of National Intelligence, "Assessing Russian Activities and Intentions in Recent U.S. Elections," January 6, 2017, https://dni.gov/files/documents /ICA_2017_01.pdf, 4.
5. Facebook estimated that roughly twenty-nine million people were served content in their news feeds directly from the IRA's eighty thousand posts from 2015 to 2017. Natasha Bertrand, "Twitter Will Tell Congress that Russia's Election Meddling Was Worse Than We First Thought," *Business Insider*, October 31, 2017, http:// businessinsider.com /twitter-russia-facebook-election-accounts-2017-10.
6. Nicholas Confessore and Daisuke Wakabayashi, "How Russia Harvested American Rage to Reshape U.S. Politics," *New York Times*, October 9, 2017, https:// nytimes.com /2017/10/09/technology/russia-election-facebook-ads-rage.html.
7. Bertrand, "Twitter Will Tell Congress"; Tim Lister, Jim Sciutto, and Mary Ilyushina, "Exclusive: Putin's 'Chef,' the Man Behind the Troll Factory," CNN, October 17, 2017, http://cnn.com/2017/10/17/politics/russian-oligarch-putin-chef-troll-factory/index .html.
8. Lawrence Norden and Ian Vandewalker, "This Bill Would Help Stop Russia From Buying Online Election Ads," *Slate*, October 19, 2017, http://slate.com/articles

/technology/future_tense/2017/10/the_honest_ads_act_would_help_stop_online
_election_meddling_from_foreign.html.

9. Geoff Mulvihill and Jake Pearson, "Federal Government Notifies 21 States of
   Election Hacking," Associated Press, September 23, 2017, https://apnews.com
   /cb8a753a9b0948589cc372a3c037a567/Federal-government-notifies-21-states-of
   -election-hacking.

10. Michael Riley and Jordan Robertson, "Russian Cyber Hacks on U.S. Electoral
    System Far Wider Than Previously Known," *Bloomberg Politics*, June 13, 2017, https://
    bloomberg.com/news/articles/2017-06-13/russian-breach-of-39-states-threatens
    -future-u-s-elections.

11. Devin Barrett and Karoun Demirjian, "How a Dubious Russian Document Influ-
    enced the FBI's Handling of the Clinton Probe," *Washington Post*, May 24, 2017, http://
    washingtonpost.com/world/national-security/how-a-dubious-russian-document
    -influenced-the-fbis-handling-of-the-clinton-probe/2017/05/24/f375c07c-3a95-11e7
    -9e48-c4f199710b69_story.html.

12. Rosalind S. Helderman and Tom Hamburger, "Top Campaign Officials Knew of
    Trump Adviser's Outreach to Russia," *Washington Post*, October 30, 2017, https://
    washingtonpost.com/politics/trump-campaign-adviser-pleaded-guilty-to-lying-about
    -russian-contacts/2017/10/30/d525e712-bd7d-11e7-97d9-bdab5a0ab381_story.html.

13. On June 7, after the offer but before the meeting, Trump announced that he planned
    to "give a major speech . . . discussing all of the things that have taken place with
    the Clintons." See Miles Parks, Tamara Keith, and Madeline Garcia, "2016 Under
    Scrutiny: A Timeline of Russia Connection," NPR, October 31, 2017, http://npr
    .org/2017/10/31/537926933/2016-under-scrutiny-a-timeline-of-russia-connections. On
    the Trump Jr.-Veselnitskaya meeting, see Ryan Lizza, "Donald Trump, Jr., Attempts to
    Explain That Russia Meeting," *New Yorker*, September 7, 2017, http://newyorker.com
    /news/ryan-lizza/donald-trump-jr-attempts-to-explain-that-russia-meeting.

14. Ashley Parker and David E. Sanger, "Donald Trump Calls on Russia to Find Hillary
    Clinton's Missing Emails," *New York Times*, July 27, 2016, https://nytimes.com/2016
    /07/28/us/politics/donald-trump-russia-clinton-emails.html.

15. Ryan Lucas, "Carter Page Tells House Intel Panel He Spoke to Sessions About Russia
    Contacts," NPR, November 7, 2017, http://npr.org/2017/11/07/562537269/inquiry
    -widens-following-disclosure-of-trump-aides-told-about-russia-contacts.

16. On August 21, 2016, Stone tweeted, "Trust me, it will soon be Podesta's time in the
    barrel, #Crooked Hillary." Podesta's stolen emails were released by WikiLeaks start-
    ing October 7, 2016. See Parks, Keith, and Garcia, "2016 Under Scrutiny."

17. Michael S. Schmidt and Nicholas Fandos, "Donald Trump Jr. Communicated With
    WikiLeaks During Campaign," *New York Times*, November 14, 2017, https://nytimes
    .com/2017/11/13/us/politics/donald-trump-jr-wikileaks-emails-democrats.html.

18. Julia Boccagno, "NSA Chief Speaks Candidly of Russia and US Election," CBS News,
    November 17, 2016.

19. The briefing by White House Homeland Security Advisor Lisa Monaco, Secre-
    tary of Homeland Security Jeh Johnson, and FBI Director James Comey to the so-
    called Gang of Twelve (a group that includes House and Senate leaders and chairs
    and ranking members of both chambers' committees on intelligence and home-
    land security) took place in September. Adam Entous, Ellen Nakashima, and Greg
    Miller, "Secret CIA Assessment Says Russia Was Trying to Help Trump Win White
    House," *Washington Post*, December 9, 2016, http://washingtonpost.com/world
    /national-security/obama-orders-review-of-russian-hacking-during-presidential
    -campaign/2016/12/09/31d6b300-be2a-11e6-94ac-3d324840106c_story.html.

20. In September 2016, Secretary of Homeland Security Jeh Johnson proposed designating state voting mechanisms "critical infrastructure," a label that would have facilitated federal assistance to states, but most state officials categorically refused. McConnell and a group of congressional leaders also expressed their opposition to "any effort by the federal government" to encroach on states' authority in a September statement that called for securing voting systems from attack but did not mention Russia (see Paul Ryan, Nancy Pelosi, Mitch McConnell, and Harry Reid, letter to Todd Valentine, president of the National Association of State Election Directors, September 28, 2016, http://politico.com/f/?id=00000157-7606-d0b2-a35f-7e1f2aac0001). See also Entous, Nakashima, and Miller, "Secret CIA Assessment."

21. John Brennan, interview by Chuck Todd, *Meet the Press*, July 9, 2017, http://nbcnews.com/feature/meet-the-press-24-7/meet-press-july-9-2017-n781106.

22. Entous, Nakashima, and Miller, "Secret CIA Assessment."

23. Department of Homeland Security, "Joint Statement From the Department of Homeland Security and Office of the Director of National Intelligence on Election Security," October 7, 2016, https://dhs.gov/news/2016/10/07/joint-statement-department-homeland-security-and-office-director-national.

24. White House Office of the Press Secretary, "Statement by the President on Actions in Response to Russian Malicious Cyber Activity and Harassment," December 29, 2016, https://obamawhitehouse.archives.gov/the-press-office/2016/12/29/statement-president-actions-response-russian-malicious-cyber-activity.

25. Noland D. McCaskill, "Trump: It's Time 'to Move On' From Claims of Russian Interference in Election," *Politico*, December 29, 2016, https://politico.com/story/2016/12/trump-russian-cyberattacks-intelligence-233045.

26. Julie Hirschfeld Davis, "Trump Tries to Shift Focus as First Charges Reportedly Loom in Russia Case," *New York Times*, October 29, 2017, http://nytimes.com/2017/10/29/us/politics/trump-clinton-mueller-russia.html.

27. Donald J. Trump, first presidential debate with Hillary Rodham Clinton, Hofstra University, Hempstead, NY, September 26, 2016.

28. Phil Stewart and Valerie Volcovici, "Trump Backtracks on Cyber Unit With Russia After Harsh Criticism," Reuters, July 9, 2017, https://reuters.com/article/us-usa-trump-russia-cyber/trump-backtracks-on-cyber-unit-with-russia-after-harsh-criticism-idUSKBN19U0P4.

29. For more on Trump's refusal to acknowledge the reality of the Russian intervention, see Greg Miller, Greg Jaffe, and Philip Rucker, "Doubting the Intelligence, Trump Pursues Putin and Leaves a Russian Threat Unchecked," *Washington Post*, December 14, 2017, https://washingtonpost.com/graphics/2017/world/national-security/donald-trump-pursues-vladimir-putin-russian-election-hacking/.

30. Trump also praised Putin as "highly respected within his country and beyond." Jeremy Diamond, "Timeline: Donald Trump's Praise for Vladimir Putin," CNN, July 29, 2016, http://cnn.com/2016/07/28/politics/donald-trump-vladimir-putin-quotes/index.html; Andrew Kaczynski, Chris Massie, and Nathan McDermott, "80 Times Trump Talked About Putin," CNN, March 2017, http://cnn.com/interactive/2017/03/politics/trump-putin-russia-timeline/.

31. Donald J. Trump, interview by Joe Scarborough, *Morning Joe*, MSNBC, December 18, 2015, http://msnbc.com/morning-joe/watch/trump--putin-is-a-leader--unlike-our-president-588186691983.

32. James Kirchick, "How Trump Got His Party to Love Russia," *Washington Post*, January 6, 2017, http://washingtonpost.com/posteverything/wp/2017/01/06/how-trump-got-his-party-to-love-russia/; Tyler Pager, "Trump to Look at Recognizing Crimea as Russian Territory, Lifting Sanctions," *Politico*, July 27, 2016, http://politico.com/story/2016/07/trump-crimea-sanctions-russia-226292; Rainer Buergin and Toluse

Olorunnipa, "Trump Slams NATO, Floats Russia Nuke Deal in European Interview," *Bloomberg Politics*, January 15, 2017, https://bloomberg.com/news/articles/2017-01-15/trump-calls-nato-obsolete-and-dismisses-eu-in-german-interview; "Donald Trump Would Consider Alliance With Russia's Vladimir Putin Against ISIS," Reuters via *Newsweek*, July 25, 2016, http://newsweek.com/donald-trump-vladimir-putin-isis-syria-iraq-moscow-islamic-state-democratic-483826.

33. Donald J. Trump (@realDonaldTrump), "When will all the haters and fools out there realize that having a good relationship with Russia is a good thing," Twitter, November 11, 2017, https://twitter.com/realdonaldtrump/status/929503641014112256.

34. Countering America's Adversaries Through Sanctions Act of 2017, Pub. L. No. 115-44.

35. For a good analysis of the law, see Daniel Fried and Brian O'Toole, "The New Russia Sanctions Law: What It Does and How to Make It Work," Issue Brief (Washington, DC: Atlantic Council, September 2017), http://atlanticcouncil.org/images/The_New_Russia_Sanctions_Law_web_0929.pdf.

36. White House Office of the Press Secretary, "Statement by President Donald J. Trump on Signing the 'Countering America's Adversaries Through Sanctions Act,'" August 2, 2017, https://whitehouse.gov/the-press-office/2017/08/02/statement-president-donald-j-trump-signing-countering-americas.

37. Robbie Gramer and Dan DeLuce, "State Department Scraps Sanctions Office," *Foreign Policy*, October 26, 2017, http://foreignpolicy.com/2017/10/26/state-department-scraps-sanctions-office/.

38. "Putin's Prepared Remarks at 43rd Munich Conference on Security Policy," *Washington Post*, February 12, 2007, http://washingtonpost.com/wp-dyn/content/article/2007/02/12/AR2007021200555.html.

39. Cindy Saine, "What's Behind Putin's Hate for the Magnitsky Act?," Voice of America, July 18, 2017, http://voanews.com/a/magnitsky-act-vladimir-putin/3949310.html.

40. Ivo H. Daalder, "Responding to Russia's Resurgence," *Foreign Affairs*, November/December 2017, 32.

41. Brian Todd and Steve Almasy, "Russia, Taliban Share Intelligence in Fight Against ISIS," CNN, December 25, 2015, http://edition.cnn.com/2015/12/24/europe/putin-taliban-isis/; Thomas Gibbons-Neff, "Russia Is Sending Weapons to Taliban, Top U.S. General Confirms," *Washington Post*, April 24, 2017, https://washingtonpost.com/news/checkpoint/wp/2017/04/24/russia-is-sending-weapons-to-taliban-top-u-s-general-confirms/; Nick Paton Walsh and Masoud Popalzai, "Videos Suggest Russian Government May Be Arming Taliban," CNN, July 26, 2017, http://cnn.com/2017/07/25/asia/taliban-weapons-afghanistan/index.html.

42. Russia initially claimed, falsely, that the exercise involved only 12,700 troops. Andrew Higgins, "Russia's War Games With Fake Enemies Cause Real Alarm," *New York Times*, September 13, 2017, https://nytimes.com/2017/09/13/world/europe/russia-baltics-belarus.html.

43. U.S. Department of State Office of the Spokesperson, "Remarks of Secretary of State Hillary Rodham Clinton, OSCE First Plenary Session," December 6, 2011, http://osce.org/mc/85930.

44. James Clapper, interview by Susan B. Glasser, *Global Politico*, October 30, 2017, https://politico.com/magazine/story/2017/10/30/james-clapper-russia-global-politico-trump-215761.

45. Graham Allison, "America and Russia: Back to Basics," *National Interest*, August 14, 2017, http://nationalinterest.org/feature/america-russia-back-basics-21901. See also James Dobbins, "Walk and Chew Gum When Dealing With Russia," *U.S. News and World Report*, August 2, 2017, https://usnews.com/opinion/world-report/articles/2017-08-02/president-donald-trump-and-congress-must-come-together-to-deal-with-russia.

46. George W. Bush, remarks at "The Spirit of Liberty: At Home, in the World," the Bush Institute's national forum, New York, NY, October 19, 2017.

47. Daniel Fried and Brian O'Toole, "Trump Administration's Significant Action on Russia Sanctions," Atlantic Council, October 27, 2017, http://atlanticcouncil.org /blogs/new-atlanticist/trump-administration-s-significant-action-on-russia-sanctions.

48. White House Office of the Press Secretary, "Presidential Executive Order on Strengthening the Cybersecurity of Federal Networks and Critical Infrastructure," May 11, 2017, https://whitehouse.gov/the-press-office/2017/05/11/presidential-executive -order-strengthening-cybersecurity-federal.

49. Ben Buchanan and Michael Sulmeyer, "Russia and Cyber Operations: Challenges and Opportunities for the Next U.S. Administration," Carnegie Endowment for International Peace, December 13, 2016, http://carnegieendowment.org/2016/12/13 /russia-and-cyber-operations-challenges-and-opportunities-for-next-u.s.-administration -pub-66433.

50. Michael Chertoff, "Congress Can Help Prevent Election Hacking," *Wall Street Journal*, September 5, 2017, https://wsj.com/articles/congress-can-help-prevent-election-hacking -1504652957; Michael McFaul, "Enough Is Enough: How to Stop Russia's Cyber Interference," *Washington Post*, September 28, 2017, http://washingtonpost.com/news /global-opinions/wp/2017/09/28/enough-is-enough-how-to-stop-russias-cyber -interference.

51. P. W. Singer, "Cyber-Deterrence and the Goal of Resilience: 30 New Actions That Congress Can Take to Improve U.S. Cybersecurity," Prepared Testimony and State-ment for the Record at the Hearing on Cyber Warfare in the 21st Century: Threats, Challenges, and Opportunities, Before the House Armed Services Committee, March 1, 2017, http://docs.house.gov/meetings/AS/AS00/20170301/105607/HHRG -115-AS00-Wstate-SingerP-20170301.pdf; Adam Segal, *Rebuilding Trust Between Sili-con Valley and Washington* (New York: Council on Foreign Relations, January 2017), https://cfr.org/report/rebuilding-trust-between-silicon-valley-and-washington.

52. Potentially useful legislative initiatives include the Honest Ads Act, sponsored by Senators Amy Klobuchar, Mark Warner, and John McCain, and the DISCLOSE Act of 2017, sponsored by Sheldon Whitehouse. See Norden and Vandewalker, "This Bill Would Help Stop Russia From Buying Online Election Ads," and Hamza Shaban and Karoun Demirjian, "Facebook and Google Might Be One Step Closer to New Regulations on Ad Transparency," *Washington Post*, October 29, 2017, http:// washingtonpost.com/news/the-switch/wp/2017/10/19/facebook-and-google-might -be-one-step-closer-to-new-regulations-on-ad-transparency/. See also Honest Ads Act, H.R. 4077, 115th Cong. (2017) and DISCLOSE Act of 2017, S. 1585, 115th Cong. (2017).

53. Foreign Agents Registration Modernization and Enforcement Act, S. 625, 115th Cong. (2017).

54. Alliance for Securing Democracy, German Marshall Fund of the United States, http:// securingdemocracy.gmfus.org.

55. "Continuing Transparency on Russian Activity," Facebook, November 22, 2017, https://newsroom.fb.com/news/2017/11/continuing-transparency-on-russian-activity/; Jon Russell, "Twitter Bans Russia Today and Sputnik From Advertising on Its Service," *TechCrunch*, October 26, 2017, https://techcrunch.com/2017/10/26/twitter-bans-russia -today-and-sputnik-from-advertising-on-its-service/; Hamza Shaban and David Filipov, "Google Is Getting Pulled Into a Fight With Russia Over RT and Sputnik," *Washington Post*, November 21, 2017, https://washingtonpost.com/news/the-switch/wp/2017/11/21 /google-is-getting-pulled-into-a-fight-with-russia-over-rt-and-sputnik/.

56. Released in April 2016, the Panama Papers were the result of a leak of millions of files from the world's fourth-biggest offshore law firm, Mossack Fonseca. The leaked

documents allegedly showed the extensive efforts of corrupt politicians all around the world, including Putin, to launder billions of dollars and keep them hidden in offshore accounts. Putin reportedly considered the leak a personal attack on him by the United States. See Luke Harding, "What Are the Panama Papers? A Guide to History's Biggest Data Leak," *Guardian*, April 3, 2016, https://theguardian.com/news/2016/apr/03/what-you-need-to-know-about-the-panama-papers; Adam Taylor, "Putin Saw the Panama Papers as a Personal Attack on Him and May Have Wanted Revenge, Russian Authors Say," *Washington Post*, August 28, 2017, https://washingtonpost.com/news/worldviews/wp/2017/08/28/putin-saw-the-panama-papers-as-a-personal-attack-and-may-have-wanted-revenge-russian-authors-say/.

57. Lisa Sawyer Samp, Kathleen H. Hicks, Olga Oliker, Jeffrey Rathke, Jeffrey Mankoff, Anthony Bell, and Heather Conley, *Recalibrating U.S. Strategy Toward Russia: A New Time for Choosing* (Washington, DC: Center for Strategic and International Studies/Rowman & Littlefield, 2017), 97, http://www.csis.org/analysis/recalibrating-us-strategy-toward-russia.

58. Daniel Fried and Brian O'Toole, "The New Russia Sanctions Law: What It Does and How to Make It Work," Atlantic Council, September 2017, 2.

59. Defense Manpower Data Center, "Military and Civilian Personnel by Service/Agency by State/Country," Department of Defense, 2008–2017, http://dmdc.osd.mil/appj/dwp/dwp_reports.jsp; United States European Command, "U.S. Military Presence in Europe (1945–2016)," May 26, 2016.

60. Such deployments would not be inconsistent with NATO pledges made in the 1997 NATO-Russia Founding Act not to permanently deploy additional substantial combat forces, because that commitment applied to the "current and foreseeable security environment," which has clearly changed. See "Founding Act on Mutual Relations, Cooperation and Security Between NATO and the Russian Federation," NATO-Russia Council, May 27, 1997, https://nato.int/nrc-website/media/59451/1997_nato_russia_founding_act.pdf.

61. Kimberly Marten, *Reducing Tensions Between Russia and NATO* (New York: Council on Foreign Relations, 2017), 30–31, https://cfr.org/report/reducing-tensions-between-russia-and-nato.

62. Samp et al., *Recalibrating U.S. Strategy*, 113–14.

63. Small Scale LNG Access Act of 2017, S. 1981, 115th Cong. (2017).

64. James Carafano et al., "U.S. Comprehensive Strategy Toward Russia," Davis Institute Special Report no. 173, Heritage Foundation, December 9, 2015, http://heritage.org/europe/report/us-comprehensive-strategy-toward-russia.

65. Marten, *Reducing Tensions Between Russia and NATO*, 34.

66. Alexander Vershbow, cited in "NATO Deputy Secretary General Discusses Risk Reduction and Military Transparency at OSCE Conference," North Atlantic Treaty Organization, October 3, 2016, http://nato.int/cps/en/natohq/news_135531.htm.

67. James Acton, "A Strategy for (Modestly Increasing the Chance of) Saving the INF Treaty," *Russia Matters*, May 11, 2017, http://russiamatters.org/analysis/strategy-modestly-increasing-chance-saving-inf-treaty. Also see Vershbow and Rose, "Russia Violated Our Nuclear Arms Treaty: Here's How We Respond," *Hill*, April 21, 2017, http://thehill.com/blogs/pundits-blog/foreign-policy/329943-russia-violated-our-nuclear-arms-treaty-heres-how-we.

68. Ibid.

69. Rex W. Tillerson, remarks at "The U.S. and Europe: Strengthening Western Alliances," The Wilson Center, Washington, DC, November 28, 2017, https://state.gov/secretary/remarks/2017/11/276002.htm.

70. Jim Mattis, press conference at NATO headquarters, Brussels, Belgium, February 16, 2017, https://defense.gov/News/Transcripts/Transcript-View/Article/1085679/press-conference-by-secretary-mattis-at-nato-headquarters-brussels-belgium/; "To Conduct a Confirmation Hearing on the Expected Nomination of Mr. James N. Mattis to Be Secretary of Defense," Senate Committee on Armed Services, Washington, DC, January 12, 2017, 87, https://armed-services.senate.gov/imo/media/doc/17-03_01-12-17.pdf. Mattis gave this response when Senator Martin Heinrich asked him, "What are the key threats to our vital interests and in what priority level?"

71. H. R. McMaster, interview by Hugh Hewitt, MSNBC, August 5, 2017, http://hughhewitt.com/national-security-advisor-general-h-r-mcmaster-msnbc-hugh/; "China, Russia Subverting Post WW II Political Economic Order," *Business Standard*, December 4, 2017, http://business-standard.com/article/pti-stories/china-russia-subverting-post-ww-ii-political-economic-order-117120401238_1.html.

72. White House, "National Security Strategy of the United States of America," December 18, 2017, 2, 14, http://whitehouse.gov/wp-content/uploads/2017/12/NSS-Final-12-18-2017-0905.pdf.

# About the Authors

**Robert D. Blackwill** is the Henry A. Kissinger senior fellow for U.S. foreign policy at the Council on Foreign Relations (CFR). He is a former deputy assistant to the president, deputy national security advisor for strategic planning, and presidential envoy to Iraq under President George W. Bush. He was U.S. ambassador to India from 2001 to 2003. From 1989 to 1990, he was special assistant to President George H.W. Bush for European and Soviet affairs. Earlier in his career, he was the U.S. ambassador to conventional arms negotiations with the Warsaw Pact, director for European affairs at the National Security Council, principal deputy assistant secretary of state for political-military affairs, and principal deputy assistant secretary of state for European affairs. Blackwill is the author and editor of many articles and books on transatlantic relations, Russia and the West, the greater Middle East, and Asian security. His latest book, *War by Other Means: Geoeconomics and Statecraft*, coauthored with Jennifer M. Harris, was named a best foreign policy book of 2016 by *Foreign Affairs*.

**Philip H. Gordon** is the Mary and David Boies senior fellow in U.S. foreign policy at CFR and a senior advisor at Albright Stonebridge Group in Washington, DC. Prior to joining CFR, Gordon served on the National Security Council staff as special assistant to the president and White House coordinator for the Middle East, North Africa, and the Gulf region from 2013 to 2015. At the White House, he worked closely with the president, secretary of state, and national security advisor on U.S. policy toward the region. From 2009 to 2013, Gordon served as assistant secretary of state for European and Eurasian affairs and was responsible for fifty countries in Europe and Eurasia as well as for the North Atlantic Treaty Organization and the European Union. He has written numerous books and articles about U.S. foreign policy and Middle East affairs and writes regularly for publications including the *New York Times*, the *Washington Post*, the *Financial Times*, *Foreign Affairs*, and *Politico*.

# Council Special Reports

*Published by the Council on Foreign Relations*

*Reducing Tensions Between Russia and NATO*
Kimberly Marten; CSR No. 79, March 2017
A Center for Preventive Action Report

*Rebuilding Trust Between Silicon Valley and Washington*
Adam Segal; CSR No. 78, January 2017

*Ending South Sudan's Civil War*
Kate Almquist Knopf; CSR No. 77, November 2016
A Center for Preventive Action Report

*Repairing the U.S.-Israel Relationship*
Robert D. Blackwill and Philip H. Gordon; CSR No. 76, November 2016

*Securing a Democratic Future for Myanmar*
Priscilla A. Clapp; CSR No. 75, March 2016
A Center for Preventive Action Report

*Xi Jinping on the Global Stage: Chinese Foreign Policy Under a Powerful but Exposed Leader*
Robert D. Blackwill and Kurt M. Campbell; CSR No. 74, February 2016
An International Institutions and Global Governance Program Report

*Enhancing U.S. Support for Peace Operations in Africa*
Paul D. Williams; CSR No. 73, May 2015

*Revising U.S. Grand Strategy Toward China*
Robert D. Blackwill and Ashley J. Tellis; CSR No. 72, March 2015
An International Institutions and Global Governance Program Report

*Strategic Stability in the Second Nuclear Age*
Gregory D. Koblentz; CSR No. 71, November 2014

*U.S. Policy to Counter Nigeria's Boko Haram*
John Campbell; CSR No. 70, November 2014
A Center for Preventive Action Report

*Limiting Armed Drone Proliferation*
Micah Zenko and Sarah Kreps; CSR No. 69, June 2014
A Center for Preventive Action Report

*Strengthening the Nuclear Nonproliferation Regime*
Paul Lettow; CSR No. 54, April 2010
An International Institutions and Global Governance Program Report

*The Russian Economic Crisis*
Jeffrey Mankoff; CSR No. 53, April 2010

*Somalia: A New Approach*
Bronwyn E. Bruton; CSR No. 52, March 2010
A Center for Preventive Action Report

*The Future of NATO*
James M. Goldgeier; CSR No. 51, February 2010
An International Institutions and Global Governance Program Report

*The United States in the New Asia*
Evan A. Feigenbaum and Robert A. Manning; CSR No. 50, November 2009
An International Institutions and Global Governance Program Report

*Intervention to Stop Genocide and Mass Atrocities: International Norms and U.S. Policy*
Matthew C. Waxman; CSR No. 49, October 2009
An International Institutions and Global Governance Program Report

*Enhancing U.S. Preventive Action*
Paul B. Stares and Micah Zenko; CSR No. 48, October 2009
A Center for Preventive Action Report

*The Canadian Oil Sands: Energy Security vs. Climate Change*
Michael A. Levi; CSR No. 47, May 2009
A Maurice R. Greenberg Center for Geoeconomic Studies Report

*The National Interest and the Law of the Sea*
Scott G. Borgerson; CSR No. 46, May 2009

*Lessons of the Financial Crisis*
Benn Steil; CSR No. 45, March 2009
A Maurice R. Greenberg Center for Geoeconomic Studies Report

*Global Imbalances and the Financial Crisis*
Steven Dunaway; CSR No. 44, March 2009
A Maurice R. Greenberg Center for Geoeconomic Studies Report

*Eurasian Energy Security*
Jeffrey Mankoff; CSR No. 43, February 2009

*Preparing for Sudden Change in North Korea*
Paul B. Stares and Joel S. Wit; CSR No. 42, January 2009
A Center for Preventive Action Report

*Averting Crisis in Ukraine*
Steven Pifer; CSR No. 41, January 2009
A Center for Preventive Action Report

*Congo: Securing Peace, Sustaining Progress*
Anthony W. Gambino; CSR No. 40, October 2008
A Center for Preventive Action Report

*Deterring State Sponsorship of Nuclear Terrorism*
Michael A. Levi; CSR No. 39, September 2008

*China, Space Weapons, and U.S. Security*
Bruce W. MacDonald; CSR No. 38, September 2008

*Sovereign Wealth and Sovereign Power: The Strategic Consequences of American Indebtedness*
Brad W. Setser; CSR No. 37, September 2008
A Maurice R. Greenberg Center for Geoeconomic Studies Report

*Securing Pakistan's Tribal Belt*
Daniel S. Markey; CSR No. 36, July 2008 (web-only release) and August 2008
A Center for Preventive Action Report

*Avoiding Transfers to Torture*
Ashley S. Deeks; CSR No. 35, June 2008

*Global FDI Policy: Correcting a Protectionist Drift*
David M. Marchick and Matthew J. Slaughter; CSR No. 34, June 2008
A Maurice R. Greenberg Center for Geoeconomic Studies Report

*Dealing with Damascus: Seeking a Greater Return on U.S.-Syria Relations*
Mona Yacoubian and Scott Lasensky; CSR No. 33, June 2008
A Center for Preventive Action Report

*Climate Change and National Security: An Agenda for Action*
Joshua W. Busby; CSR No. 32, November 2007
A Maurice R. Greenberg Center for Geoeconomic Studies Report

*Planning for Post-Mugabe Zimbabwe*
Michelle D. Gavin; CSR No. 31, October 2007
A Center for Preventive Action Report

*The Case for Wage Insurance*
Robert J. LaLonde; CSR No. 30, September 2007
A Maurice R. Greenberg Center for Geoeconomic Studies Report

*Reform of the International Monetary Fund*
Peter B. Kenen; CSR No. 29, May 2007
A Maurice R. Greenberg Center for Geoeconomic Studies Report

*Nuclear Energy: Balancing Benefits and Risks*
Charles D. Ferguson; CSR No. 28, April 2007

*Nigeria: Elections and Continuing Challenges*
Robert I. Rotberg; CSR No. 27, April 2007
A Center for Preventive Action Report

*The Economic Logic of Illegal Immigration*
Gordon H. Hanson; CSR No. 26, April 2007
A Maurice R. Greenberg Center for Geoeconomic Studies Report

*The United States and the WTO Dispute Settlement System*
Robert Z. Lawrence; CSR No. 25, March 2007
A Maurice R. Greenberg Center for Geoeconomic Studies Report

*Bolivia on the Brink*
Eduardo A. Gamarra; CSR No. 24, February 2007
A Center for Preventive Action Report

*After the Surge: The Case for U.S. Military Disengagement From Iraq*
Steven N. Simon; CSR No. 23, February 2007

*Darfur and Beyond: What Is Needed to Prevent Mass Atrocities*
Lee Feinstein; CSR No. 22, January 2007

*Avoiding Conflict in the Horn of Africa: U.S. Policy Toward Ethiopia and Eritrea*
Terrence Lyons; CSR No. 21, December 2006
A Center for Preventive Action Report

*Living with Hugo: U.S. Policy Toward Hugo Chávez's Venezuela*
Richard Lapper; CSR No. 20, November 2006
A Center for Preventive Action Report

*Reforming U.S. Patent Policy: Getting the Incentives Right*
Keith E. Maskus; CSR No. 19, November 2006
A Maurice R. Greenberg Center for Geoeconomic Studies Report

*Foreign Investment and National Security: Getting the Balance Right*
Alan P. Larson and David M. Marchick; CSR No. 18, July 2006
A Maurice R. Greenberg Center for Geoeconomic Studies Report

*Challenges for a Postelection Mexico: Issues for U.S. Policy*
Pamela K. Starr; CSR No. 17, June 2006 (web-only release) and November 2006

*U.S.-India Nuclear Cooperation: A Strategy for Moving Forward*
Michael A. Levi and Charles D. Ferguson; CSR No. 16, June 2006

*Generating Momentum for a New Era in U.S.-Turkey Relations*
Steven A. Cook and Elizabeth Sherwood-Randall; CSR No. 15, June 2006

*Peace in Papua: Widening a Window of Opportunity*
Blair A. King; CSR No. 14, March 2006
A Center for Preventive Action Report

*Neglected Defense: Mobilizing the Private Sector to Support Homeland Security*
Stephen E. Flynn and Daniel B. Prieto; CSR No. 13, March 2006

*Afghanistan's Uncertain Transition From Turmoil to Normalcy*
Barnett R. Rubin; CSR No. 12, March 2006
A Center for Preventive Action Report

*Preventing Catastrophic Nuclear Terrorism*
Charles D. Ferguson; CSR No. 11, March 2006

*Getting Serious About the Twin Deficits*
Menzie D. Chinn; CSR No. 10, September 2005
A Maurice R. Greenberg Center for Geoeconomic Studies Report

*Both Sides of the Aisle: A Call for Bipartisan Foreign Policy*
Nancy E. Roman; CSR No. 9, September 2005

*Forgotten Intervention? What the United States Needs to Do in the Western Balkans*
Amelia Branczik and William L. Nash; CSR No. 8, June 2005
A Center for Preventive Action Report

*A New Beginning: Strategies for a More Fruitful Dialogue with the Muslim World*
Craig Charney and Nicole Yakatan; CSR No. 7, May 2005

*Power-Sharing in Iraq*
David L. Phillips; CSR No. 6, April 2005
A Center for Preventive Action Report

*Giving Meaning to "Never Again": Seeking an Effective Response to the Crisis in Darfur and Beyond*
Cheryl O. Igiri and Princeton N. Lyman; CSR No. 5, September 2004

*Freedom, Prosperity, and Security: The G8 Partnership with Africa: Sea Island 2004 and Beyond*
J. Brian Atwood, Robert S. Browne, and Princeton N. Lyman; CSR No. 4, May 2004

*Addressing the HIV/AIDS Pandemic: A U.S. Global AIDS Strategy for the Long Term*
Daniel M. Fox and Princeton N. Lyman; CSR No. 3, May 2004
Cosponsored with the Milbank Memorial Fund

*Challenges for a Post-Election Philippines*
Catharin E. Dalpino; CSR No. 2, May 2004
A Center for Preventive Action Report

*Stability, Security, and Sovereignty in the Republic of Georgia*
David L. Phillips; CSR No. 1, January 2004
A Center for Preventive Action Report

*Note:* Council Special Reports are available for download from CFR's website, CFR.org.
For more information, email publications@cfr.org.

www.ingramcontent.com/pod-product-compliance
Lightning Source LLC
Chambersburg PA
CBHW060524280326
41933CB00014B/3094